Did Dad nap?

Written by Abbie Rushton

Illustrated by Liliana Perez

Collins

Dad sits. Dad naps.

tap tap tap

pat pat pat

Dad sits in it!

Dad sits. Dad naps.

Tim dips in.

Tim pats it.

Pat it at Dad.

Tap it. Pat it.

Pat it. Tap it.

Sit in a pit.

Dad sits. Dad naps!

/d/

14

After reading

Letters and Sounds: Phase 2

Word count: 44

Focus phonemes: /s/ /a/ /t/ /p/ /i/ /n/ /m/ /d/

Curriculum links: Personal, Social and Emotional Development

Early learning goals: Reading: read and understand simple sentences; use phonic knowledge to decode regular words and read them aloud accurately

Developing fluency

- Your child may enjoy hearing you read the book.
- Take turns to read a page aloud. Read with humour to encourage expressive reading.

Phonic practice

- Turn to page 2. Ask your child to sound out the letter in each word in the first sentence, then blend. (D/a/d – **Dad** s/i/t/s – **sits**)
- On page 7, focus on the words, **Tim** and **in**. Ask your child to sound out and blend each word, checking they don't muddle the sounds /m/ in **Tim** and /n/ in **in**.
- Look at the "I spy sounds" pages (14–15). Point to and sound out the /d/ at the top of page 14, then point to the dog digging on page 15 and say "dig", emphasising the /d/ sound. Ask your child to find other things that start with the /d/ sound. (*dog*, *dad*, *doll*, *doughnut*, *drink*, *dots*). Repeat for the /s/ sound. (*sand*, *starfish*, *sun*, *suntan lotion*, *swim*, *sandcastle*, *sea*)

Extending vocabulary

- Ask your child:
  - What word could we use instead of **naps** on page 6? (e.g. *sleeps*, *dozes*)